Decadent Bundts

Bundt Recipe Book with Confirmed Delicious Bundt Recipes

By

Martha Stone

License Notes

Table of Contents

Introduction

Bundt cakes are the epitome of quality baking. Not everybody can prepare bundt cakes from the comfort of their own home. In order to make bundt cakes, one must understand the flavor, moistness and decadence needed in order to prepare a homemade bundt cake. Luckily for you, making bundt cakes are incredibly easy to prepare, as long as you have the right tools and mindset in order to do so.

That is exactly what you will discover inside of this cookbook. Throughout the pages of this cookbook, you will discover how to prepare homemade bundt cakes from your home. By the end of this cookbook, it is my hope that not only do you discover what it takes to capture the beauty that makes up a bundt cake, but feel confident to make these specialty cakes within your home. So, what are you waiting for? Let's get to baking!

Kentucky Butter Bundt Cake

This is one of the most tender, moist and delicious bundt cakes you can make whenever you need something simple.

Makes: 12 servings

Total Prep Time: 1 hour and 20 minutes

Ingredients for the cake:

- 3 cups of cake flour
- 1 tsp. of salt
- 1 tsp. of baking powder
- ½ tsp. of baking soda
- 2 cups of white sugar
- 1 cup of butter, soft
- 4 eggs
- 1 cup of buttermilk
- 2 tsp. of pure vanilla

Ingredients for the butter sauce:

- ¾ cup of white sugar
- 1/3 cup of butter
- 3 Tbsp. of water
- 2 tsp. of pure vanilla

Ingredients for the glaze:

- 1 ¼ cup of powdered sugar
- ¼ cup of butter, melted
- 2 Tbsp. of whole milk

Directions:

1. Preheat the oven to 325 degrees. Grease a bundt cake pan with cooking spray.
2. Prepare the cake. In a bowl, add in the cake flour, dash of salt, baking powder and soda. Stir well to mix.
3. In a separate bowl, add in the butter. Beat with an electric mixer for 1 to 2 minutes or until fluffy in consistency. Add in the white sugar, buttermilk and pure vanilla. Continue to beat for 1 minute or until mixed. Add in the flour mix. Beat well until incorporated.

4. Pour into the bundt cake pan.
5. Place into the oven to bake for 1 hour or until baked through. Remove and set aside.
6. Prepare the butter sauce. In a saucepan set over medium heat, add in the white sugar, butter, water and pure vanilla. Whisk until mixed. Remove from heat.
7. Poke hole over the cake. Pour the sauce over the top of the cake. Set aside to cool completely.
8. Prepare the glaze. In a bowl, add in the powdered sugar, melted butter and whole milk. Whisk until smooth in consistency. Drizzle over the top of the cake. Allow to rest for 10 minutes or until the glaze is set.
9. Serve.

Cranberry and Orange Bundt Cake

This is a summer time bundt cake you can make during your next summer celebration. This is a cake you can make to satisfy everybody's sweet tooth.

Makes: 12 servings

Total Prep Time: 1 hour and 15 minutes

Ingredients for the cake:

- 1 ½ cups of cake flour
- 2 tsp. of baking powder
- ¼ tsp. of salt
- 1 cup of sour cream
- 1 cup of white sugar
- 3 eggs
- 1 Tbsp. of orange zest
- 1 orange, juice
- ½ cup of butter
- 2 Tbsp. of white sugar
- 1 ½ cups of cranberries

Ingredients for the icing:

- 1 cup of powdered sugar
- 2 to 3 Tbsp. of water

Directions:

1. Preheat the oven to 350 degrees. Grease a bundt cake pan and dust lightly with 2 tablespoons of white sugar.
2. Sprinkle ¼ cup of the cranberries into the bundt cake pan.
3. Prepare the cake. In a bowl, add in the butter and remaining white sugar. Beat with an electric mixer until creamy in consistency. Add in the eggs, orange juice, orange zest and sour cream. Continue to beat until evenly mixed.
4. Add in the cake flour, dash of salt and baking powder. Beat well until evenly just mixed. Add in 1 ¼ cups cranberries. Fold gently to incorporate.
5. Pour into the bundt cake pan.
6. Place into the oven to bake for 50 to 55 minutes or until baked through. Remove and set aside to cool completely.

7. Prepare the icing. In a bowl, add in the powdered sugar and water. Whisk until smooth in consistency. Drizzle over the top of the cake.
8. Slice and serve.

Oreo Bundt Cake

This is a delicious bundt cake that is perfect to make for those picky eaters in your home. It is made with a chocolate cake and topped with a rich chocolate ganache.

Makes: 10 servings

Total Prep Time: 1 hour and 15 minutes

Ingredients for the cake:

- 1 box of chocolate cake mix
- 1 box of cookies and cream pudding mix
- 4 eggs
- 1 cup of low fat sour cream
- ¼ cup of vegetable oil
- 20 Oreo cookies, 8 cookies whole and remaining chopped

Ingredients for the ganache:

- 1 cup of semi-sweet chocolate chips
- ¼ cup of heavy whipping cream
- 3 Tbsp. of butter

Ingredients for the frosting:

- 1 box of cookies and cream pudding mix
- ¾ cup of heavy whipping cream
- 1, 8 ounce container of whipped topping

Directions:

1. Prepare the cake. In a bowl, add in the cake mix, cookies and cream pudding mix, sour cream, vegetable oil, eggs and half of the chopped Oreos. Stir well to mix.
2. Grease a bundt cake pan with cooking spray.
3. Spread half of the batter into the bundt pan. Add 8 whole Oreos over the batter. Spread the remaining batter over the top.
4. Place into the oven to bake for 40 to 45 minutes at 350 degrees or until baked through. Remove and set aside to cool completely.
5. Prepare the ganache. In a bowl, add in the semi-sweet chocolate chips, heavy whipping cream and butter. Microwave for 30 seconds or until melted. Stir well until smooth in consistency. Drizzle over the top of the bundt cake. Set aside to rest for 10 to 15 minutes or until set.

6. Prepare the frosting. In a bowl, add in the cookies and cream pudding mix and heavy whipping cream. Whisk until smooth in consistency. Add in the whipped topping. Fold until incorporated. Spread over the top of the cake.
7. Sprinkle the remaining Oreos over the top.
8. Slice and serve.

Italian Cream Bundt Cake

This is a bundt cake made with a combination of coconut, cream cheese and chopped pecans to make a decadent dessert dish.

Makes: 10 to 12 servings

Total Prep Time: 1 hour and 30 minutes

Ingredients for the cake:

- 1 cup of pecans, chopped
- 1 cup of sweetened coconut, shredded
- 3 cups of cake flour
- 1 tsp. of baking powder
- ½ tsp. of salt
- 1 cup of butter, soft
- 1 cup of white sugar
- 1 cup of light brown sugar
- 4 eggs
- 1 tsp. of pure vanilla
- 1 cup of whole milk

Ingredients for the glaze:

- 4 ounces of cream cheese
- 1 cup of powdered sugar
- ½ tsp. of pure vanilla
- 2 to 3 Tbsp. of whole milk

Directions:

1. Preheat the oven to 350 degrees. Add a sheet of parchment paper onto a baking sheet. Grease a bundt cake pan and dust lightly with flour.
2. Spread the chopped pecans onto the baking sheet. Place into the oven to bake for 10 to 15 minutes or until browned. Remove and set aside.
3. Prepare the cake. In a bowl, add in the cake flour, dash of salt and baking powder. Stir well to mix.
4. In a separate bowl, add in the butter, white sugar and light brown sugar. Beat with an electric mixer until fluffy. Add in the eggs, pure vanilla and whole milk. Continue to beat until mixed. Add in the flour mix until incorporated.
5. Pour into the bundt cake pan.
6. Place into the oven to bake for 1 hour or until baked through. Remove and set aside to cool completely.

7. Prepare the glaze. In a bowl, add in the cream cheese, powdered sugar and pure vanilla. Beat with an electric mixer until smooth in consistency. Add in the whole milk. Continue to beat until smooth. Drizzle over the top of the cake.
8. Sprinkle the toasted pecans and coconut over the top.
9. Slice and serve.

Cream Cheese Pound Bundt Cake

If you are looking for the perfect dessert to serve to your friends and family, then this is the perfect Bundt cake for you to make.

Makes: 12 to 18 servings

Total Prep Time: 1 hour and 35 minutes

Ingredients:

- 1, 8 ounce pack of cream cheese
- 1 ½ cups of butter, soft
- 3 cups of white sugar
- 6 eggs
- 3 cups of cake flour
- 2 tsp. of pure vanilla
- Powdered sugar, for dusting
- Whipped cream, for topping
- Mixed berries, for garnish

Directions:

1. Heat the oven to 325 degrees. Spray a bundt pan with cooking spray. Dust lightly with flour.
2. In a bowl, add in the butter and cream cheese. Beat with an electric mixer until smooth in consistency. Add in the white flour. Continue to beat until fluffy in consistency.
3. Add in the eggs, cake flour and pure vanilla. Beat until just mixed.
4. Pour into the bundt cake pan.
5. Place into the oven to bake for 1 hour and 20 minutes or until baked through. Remove and set aside to cool completely.
6. Dust the powdered sugar over the top of the cake.
7. Serve with the whipped cream and mixed berries.

Chocolate and Peanut Butter Bundt Cake

This is a bundt cake that incorporates the flavors of two of your favorite flavors to make one epic dessert that you will love.

Makes: 8 servings

Total Prep Time: 1 hour and 15 minutes

Ingredients for the cake:

- 3 cups of cake flour
- 2 tsp. of baking powder
- ½ tsp. of baking soda
- Dash of salt
- 1 cup of butter, soft
- 2 ½ cups of white sugar
- 3 eggs
- 1 cup of sour cream
- 2 tsp. of pure vanilla
- 1 ¼ cups of whole milk
- 5 ounces of bittersweet chocolate, melted
- 1 cup of creamy peanut butter

Ingredients for the glaze:

- 1 ¼ cups of powdered sugar
- 1/3 cup of creamy peanut butter
- 4 to 5 Tbsp. of half and half

Directions:

1. Preheat the oven to 350 degrees. Grease a bundt cake pan and dust lightly with flour.
2. Prepare the cake. In a bowl, add in the cake flour, dash of salt, baking powder and soda. Stir well to mix.
3. In a bowl of a stand mixer, add in the white sugar and butter. Beat on the medium setting until creamy in consistency. Add in the eggs, sour cream and pure vanilla. Continue to beat until mixed.
4. Add in the flour mix and beat well until just mixed.
5. Pour half of the batter into a separate bowl. Add in the melted chocolate into one half of the batter. In the second half of the batter, add in the creamy peanut butter.
6. Spread both batters into the bundt cake pan in layers. Swirl around with a knife.
7. Place into the oven to bake for 1 hour or until baked through. Remove and set aside to cool completely.

8. Prepare the glaze. In a bowl, add in the powdered sugar, creamy peanut butter and half and half. Whisk until smooth in consistency. Drizzle over the top of the cake.
9. Slice and serve.

Decadent Chocolate Bundt Cake

This is the perfect bundt cake that is perfect for all of those chocoholics in your home. It is packed full of a rich chocolate flavor that is hard to resist.

Makes: 12 servings

Total Prep Time: 1 hour and 30 minutes

Ingredients:

- 1 ¼ cups + 1 Tbsp. of coffee, brewed
- ¾ cup of powdered cocoa
- 2 ¼ cups of white sugar
- 1 ¼ tsp. of salt
- 2 ½ tsp. of baking soda
- 2 egg
- 1 egg yolk
- 1 ¼ cups + 1 Tbsp. of buttermilk
- 1 cup + 2 Tbsp. of canola oil
- 1 ½ tsp. of pure vanilla
- 1 cup + 2 Tbsp. of cake flour

Ingredients for the glaze:

- 3 ounces of unsweetened chocolate, chopped
- 6 Tbsp. of butter
- 1 ½ cups of powdered sugar
- ¼ cup of sour cream
- 1/8 cup of coffee, brewed

Directions:

1. Preheat the oven to 350 degrees. Grease a bundt pan and dust lightly with flour.
2. Prepare the cake. In a saucepan set over medium heat, add in the powdered cocoa and brewed coffee. Allow to come to a boil. Remove from heat. Set aside to rest for 30 minutes.
3. In a stand mixer, add in the white sugar, dash of salt, eggs, egg yolk, coffee mix and baking soda. Beat well to mix. Add in the buttermilk, canola oil and pure vanilla. Continue to beat until mixed. Add in the cake flour. Mix for 3 minutes or until blended.
4. Pour into the cake pan.
5. Place into the oven to bake for 1 hour or until baked through. Remove and set aside to cool completely.
6. In a separate bowl, prepare the glaze. In a bowl set over a saucepan filled with simmering water, add in the chopped chocolate. Whisk until melted. Add in the butter, powdered sugar, sour cream and brewed coffee. Continue to whisk until thick in consistency.
7. Pour the glaze over the top of the cake.

8. Set the cake aside to rest for 1 hour or until set.

9. Slice and serve.

Funfetti Bundt Cake

This is a delicious bundt cake that is perfect to serve for those birthday celebrations. It is topped with a simple glaze and plenty of sprinkles, everybody will be raving about this cake.

Makes: 10 servings

Total Prep Time: 1 hour

Ingredients for the cake:

- 1 ½ cups of cake flour
- ½ tsp. of baking soda
- Dash of salt
- ¼ cup of whole milk
- ½ cup of sour cream
- ½ cup of butter, soft
- ¾ cup of white sugar
- 2 eggs
- ½ tsp. of pure vanilla
- ¼ cup of rainbow sprinkles

Ingredients for the glaze:

- 2 cups of powdered sugar
- 2 Tbsp. of whole milk
- 1 drop of fushia food coloring

Directions:

1. Preheat the oven to 325 degrees. Grease a bundt cake pan and dust lightly with flour.
2. Prepare the cake. In a bowl, add in the cake flour, dash of salt, rainbow sprinkles and baking soda. Stir well to mix and set this mix aside.
3. In a separate bowl, add in the whole milk and sour cream. Stir well to mix.
4. In a separate bowl, add in the butter and white sugar. Beat with an electric mixer until fluffy. Add in the eggs, pure vanilla and milk mix. Beat well until mixed. Add in the flour mix. Beat well until just mixed.
5. Pour into the bundt cake pan.
6. Place into the oven to bake for 35 to 40 minutes or until baked through. Remove and set aside to cool completely.

7. Prepare the glaze. In a bowl, add in the powdered sugar, whole milk and food coloring. Whisk until smooth in consistency. Drizzle over the top of the cake.
8. Allow the cake to rest for 20 minutes or until set.
9. Slice and serve.

Shirley Temple Bundt Cake

This is a perfect bundt cake to make whenever you want to live your best childhood moments. Topped off with a cherry sugar glaze, this is a cake dish that will satisfy any sweet tooth.

Makes: 12 servings

Total Prep Time: 1 hour and 45 minutes

Ingredients for the cake:

- 1 ½ cups of butter
- 3 cups of white sugar
- 5 eggs
- 3 cups of cake flour
- 2 tsp. of lemon extract
- ¾ cup of seven up
- 10 ounces of maraschino cherries, drained and juice reserved

Ingredients for the glaze:

- 2 cups of powdered sugar
- 1 tsp. of lemon extract
- 3 to 4 Tbsp. of whole milk

Directions:

1. Preheat the oven to 325 degrees.
2. Prepare the cake. In a bowl, add in the butter and white sugar. Beat with an electric mixer until fluffy in consistency. Add in the eggs, cake flour, lemon extract, seven up and drained cherries. Beat on the lowest setting until just mixed.
3. Pour into a greased bundt cake pan.
4. Place into the oven to bake for 1 ½ hours or until the cake is baked through. Remove and set aside to cool completely.
5. Poke holes over the entire surface of the cake using a fork. Pour the reserved cherry juice over the top.
6. Prepare the glaze. In a bowl, add in the powdered sugar, lemon extract and whole milk. Whisk until smooth in consistency. Drizzle over the top of the cake.
7. Slice and serve.

Nutella Bundt Cake

This is the perfect bundt cake to make for those who are craving Nutella. It is the perfect to make whenever you want to indulge yourself with something delicious.

Makes: 8 servings

Total Prep Time: 1 hour

Ingredients for the cake:

- 1 box of chocolate cake mix
- 1, 3.9 ounce box of chocolate pudding
- ½ cup of sour cream
- ½ cup of Nutella
- ¾ cup of vegetable oil
- ¾ cup of water
- ½ cup of white sugar
- 4 eggs
- 1 tsp. of pure vanilla

Ingredients for the frosting:

- 8 ounces of cream cheese, soft
- 2 cups of powdered sugar
- ¼ cup of Nutella
- Hazelnuts, chopped and for garnish

Directions:

1. Preheat the oven to 350 degrees. Grease a bundt cake pan and dust lightly with flour.
2. Prepare the cake. In a bowl, add in all of the ingredients for the cake mix. Beat with an electric mixer until smooth in consistency.
3. Pour into the bundt cake pan.
4. Place into the oven to bake for 45 to 50 minutes or until baked through. Remove and set aside to cool completely.
5. Prepare the frosting. In a bowl, add in the cream cheese, sugar and Nutella. Beat with an electric mixer until creamy in consistency.
6. Pipe the frosting over the top of the bundt cake.
7. Sprinkle the chopped hazelnuts over the top.
8. Slice and serve.

Lemon and Blueberry Bundt Cake

This is a delicious bundt cake you can make any time during the summer holidays. It is perfect to make for practically any occasion.

Makes: 12 servings

Total Prep Time: 1 hour

Ingredients for the cake:

- 2 ½ cups of cake flour
- ¾ tsp. of baking powder
- ¼ tsp. of baking soda
- Dash of salt
- 10 Tbsp. of butter, soft
- 1 ¼ cups of white sugar
- 1 Tbsp. of lemon zest
- 2 eggs
- 1 cup of buttermilk
- 2 Tbsp. of lemon juice
- 1 tsp. of pure vanilla
- 1 1/3 cups of blueberries

Ingredients for the glaze:

- ½ Tbsp. of butter, melted
- ½ cup of powdered sugar
- Dash of salt
- 1 tsp. of lemon zest
- 1 Tbsp. of lemon juice
- 1 tsp. of whole milk

Directions:

1. Preheat the oven to 350 degrees. Grease a bundt pan.
2. Prepare the cake. In a bowl, add in the cake flour, dash of salt, baking powder and soda. Stir well to mix. Set aside 1 tablespoon of the flour mix aside in a separate bowl with the blueberries. Toss to mix.
3. In a separate bowl, add in the butter, white sugar and lemon zest. Beat with an electric mixer until fluffy in consistency. Add in the eggs, buttermilk, lemon juice and pure vanilla. Continue to beat until mixed. Add in the flour mix and beat gently until just mixed.
4. Add in the blueberries and fold gently to incorporate.
5. Pour into the bundt pan. Place into the oven to bake for 50 minutes or until baked through. Remove and set aside to cool completely.
6. Prepare the glaze. In a bowl, add in the melted butter, powdered sugar, dash of salt, lemon zest, lemon juice and whole milk. Whisk until smooth in consistency. Drizzle over the top of the cake.
7. Slice and serve.

Sugar Cookie Bundt Cake

This is a soft and tender bundt cake that is packed full a frosted cookie flavor that even the pickiest of eaters will fall in love with.

Makes: 12 servings

Total Prep Time: 1 hour and 40 minutes

Ingredients:

- 1 cup of butter, soft
- 2 cups of white sugar
- 1 tsp. of salt
- 4 eggs
- 2 tsp. of baking powder
- 3 cups of cake flour
- 1 cup of half and half
- 1 tsp. of pure vanilla
- 1, 8 ounce block of cream cheese
- ¼ cup of butter, soft
- 2 ½ cups of powdered sugar
- Dash of salt
- 3 tsp. of half and half
- ¼ to ½ cup of rainbow sprinkles

Directions:

1. Preheat the oven to 350 degrees. Grease a bundt cake pan and dust lightly with flour.
2. In the bowl of a stand mixer, add in the 1 cup of butter and white sugar. Beat on the highest setting until fluffy in consistency. Add in the dash of salt, eggs, cake flour, baking powder, half and half and pure vanilla. Continue to beat until smooth in consistency.
3. Pour into the bundt cake pan.
4. Place into the oven to bake for 1 hour or until baked through. Remove and set aside to cool completely.
5. Prepare the frosting. In a bowl, add in the cream cheese and butter. Beat with an electric mixer until smooth. Add in the powdered sugar, dash of salt and half and half. Continue to beat until fluffy. Spread over the top of the cake.
6. Sprinkle the rainbow sprinkles over the top of the cake.
7. Slice and serve.

Strawberry Shortcake Bundt Cake

This is the perfect bundt cake to make for those special occasions. It is so delicious, I guarantee your friends and family will be impressed with your baking skills.

Makes: 12 servings

Total Prep Time: 4 hours and 15 minutes

Ingredients for the cake:

- 1 box of yellow cake mix
- 1 cup of whole milk
- 4 ounces of cream cheese, soft
- 3 eggs

Ingredients for the strawberry mix:

- 1 ½ cups of strawberries, thinly sliced
- ¼ cup of white sugar
- 2 tsp. of lemon juice

Ingredients for the glaze:

- ¾ cups of powdered sugar
- 2 Tbsp. of butter, soft
- 1 ounce of cream cheese, soft
- 1 to 2 Tbsp. of whole milk
- ¼ tsp. of pure vanilla

Directions:

1. Preheat the oven to 325 degrees. Grease a bundt cake and dust lightly with flour.
2. Prepare the cake. In a bowl, add in the yellow cake mix, whole milk, soft cream cheese and eggs. Beat with an electric mixer until mixed.
3. Pour into the bundt cake pan.
4. Place into the oven to bake for 45 minutes or until baked through. Remove and set aside to cool completely.
5. Prepare the strawberry mix. In a blender, add in the sliced strawberries, white sugar and lemon juice. Blend on the highest setting until smooth in consistency. Poke holes all over the cake using a fork. Pour the strawberry mix over the top of the cake.
6. Prepare the glaze. In a bowl, add in the powdered sugar, soft butter, cream cheese, whole milk and pure vanilla. Whisk until smooth in consistency. Drizzle over the top of the cake.
7. Slice and serve.

Caramel Apple Bundt Cake

This is the perfect bundt cake to make right in time for the Thanksgiving season. It is a dish your family will be begging for the recipe for.

Makes: 8 servings

Total Prep Time: 1 hour and 40 minutes

Ingredients for the cake:

- 3 cups of cake flour
- 1 tsp. of baking soda
- 2 tsp. of powdered cinnamon
- ½ tsp. of powdered nutmeg
- Dash of salt
- 3 apples, chopped
- 1 Tbsp. of lemon juice
- 3 Tbsp. of light brown sugar
- 2 tsp. of pure vanilla, evenly divided
- 1 ¼ cups of vegetable oil
- 2 cups of white sugar
- 3 eggs

Ingredients for the cream cheese:

- 8 ounces of cream cheese
- 1/3 cup of white sugar
- ½ tsp. of pure vanilla
- 1 egg

Ingredients for the glaze:

- 2 Tbsp. of butter
- 2 Tbsp. of light brown sugar
- 2 Tbsp. of white sugar
- 2 Tbsp. of heavy whipping cream
- 1 tsp. of pure vanilla

Ingredients for the caramel:

- 4 Tbsp. of butter
- 1 cup of light brown sugar
- ½ cup of half and half
- Dash of salt
- 1 Tbsp. of pure vanilla

Directions:

1. Preheat the oven to 350 degrees. Grease a bundt cake pan and dust lightly with flour.

2. Prepare the cake. In a bowl, add in the cake flour, powdered cinnamon, powdered nutmeg, dash of salt and baking soda. Stir well to mix.
3. In a separate bowl, add in the apples and lemon juice. Toss well to coat. Add in the light dark sugar and 1 teaspoon of pure vanilla. Toss well to mix. Set this mix aside.
4. In a bowl of a stand mixer, add in the vegetable oil, white sugar and pure vanilla. Add in the eggs and beat well to mix. Add in the flour mix. Beat well until just mixed. Add in the apple mix. Fold gently to incorporate.
5. Pour into the cake pan.
6. Prepare the cream cheese. In a bowl, add in the cream cheese. Beat with an electric mixer for 1 minute or until smooth in consistency. Add in the white sugar, pure vanilla and egg. Continue to beat until creamy in consistency.

7. Pour the cream cheese mix over the batter in the cake pan.
8. Place into the oven to bake for 1 hour and 15 minutes or until baked through. Remove and set aside to cool completely.
9. Prepare the glaze. In a saucepan set over medium to high heat, add in all of the ingredients for the glaze. Stir well to mix. Allow to come to a boil. Remove from heat. Pour immediately over the bundt cake.
10. Prepare the caramel. In a separate saucepan set over low to medium heat, add in the butter, light brown sugar, half and half and dash of salt. Allow to come to a simmer. Whisk for 8 minutes or until thick in consistency. Add in the pure vanilla. Cook for an additional minute.
11. Drizzle the caramel over the top of the cake.
12. Slice and serve.

Eggnog Bundt Cake

This is the perfect bundt cake to serve just in time for the Christmas holidays. It is so delicious, it will become a staple in your home every Christmas.

Makes: 12 servings

Total Prep Time: 40 minutes

Ingredients for the cake:

- 3 ¼ cups of cake flour
- 1 Tbsp. of baking powder
- 1 tsp. of salt
- ¼ tsp. of powdered cinnamon
- 1/8 tsp. of powdered nutmeg
- 1 ½ cups of silky eggnog
- 3 eggs
- ½ cup of extra virgin olive oil
- 2 tsp. of pure vanilla
- 1 ¼ cup of white sugar

Ingredients for the icing:

- 2 cups of powdered sugar
- 2 Tbsp. of silky eggnog
- 1 tsp. of pure vanilla
- Dash of powdered nutmeg

Directions:

1. Preheat your oven to 350 degrees. Grease a bundt cake pan and lightly dust with the flour. 2. Prepare the cake. In a bowl, add in the cake flour, baking powder, dash of salt, powdered cinnamon and powdered nutmeg. Stir well to mix.
2. In a separate bowl, add in the eggnog, eggs, extra virgin olive oil and pure vanilla. Whisk until lightly beaten. Add into the flour mix and stir well until just mixed.
3. Pour into the bundt cake pan.
4. Place into the oven to bake for 40 minutes or until baked through. Remove and set aside to cool completely.
5. Prepare the glaze. In a bowl, add in the powdered sugar, eggnog and pure vanilla. Whisk until smooth in consistency. Drizzle over the top of the cake.
6. Sprinkle a dash of powdered nutmeg over the top.
7. Slice and serve.

Simple Lemon Bundt Cake

This is perhaps one of the softest and moist bundt cakes you will ever have the pleasure of trying. It will soon become a favorite in your household.

Makes: 12 to 16 servings

Total Prep Time: 50 minutes

Ingredients for the cake:

- 2 ¼ cups of cake flour
- 2 ¼ tsp. of baking powder
- ½ tsp. of salt
- 4 eggs
- 2 cups of white sugar
- 1 tsp. of pure vanilla
- 2 Tbsp. of lemon zest
- 2 Tbsp. + 2 tsp. of lemon juice
- 1 ¼ cups of whole milk
- 10 Tbsp. of butter, cut into cubes

Ingredients for the glaze:

- 1 ½ cups of powdered sugar
- 3 to 5 Tbsp. of lemon juice
- Ingredients for the topping:
- 1 Tbsp. of lemon zest
- 1 Tbsp. of white sugar

Directions:

1. Preheat the oven to 350 degrees. Grease a bundt cake pan and dust lightly with flour.
2. Prepare the cake. In a bowl, add in the cake flour, dash of salt and baking powder. Stir well to mix.
3. In the bowl of a stand mixer, add in the eggs. Beat on the highest setting until thick in consistency. Add in the white sugar. Continue to beat until fluffy in consistency. Add in the pure vanilla, lemon juice and lemon juice. Beat well to mix. Add in the flour mix and beat until just mixed.

4. In a saucepan set over medium heat, add in the milk. Allow to come to a simmer. Pour into the batter and stir well to mix.
5. Pour into the bundt pan.
6. Place into the oven to bake for 30 to 35 minutes or until baked through. Remove and set aside to cool completely.
7. Prepare the glaze. In a bowl, add in the lemon juice and powdered sugar. Whisk until smooth in consistency. Drizzle over the top of the bundt cake.
8. Prepare the topping. In a bowl, add in the lemon zest and white sugar. Stir to mix. Sprinkle over the top of the glaze.
9. Slice and serve.

Pumpkin Spiced Latte Bundt Cake

If you love the taste of homemade pumpkin spiced lattes, then this is the perfect bundt cake for you to prepare.

Makes: 20 servings

Total Prep Time: 1 hour and 5 minutes

Ingredients for the cake:

- 2 ½ cups of cake flour
- 2 tsp. of baking powder
- 2 tsp. of pumpkin pie spice
- 2 tsp. of powdered espresso
- 1 tsp. of salt
- ¾ cup of butter
- 1 cup of white sugar
- 1 cup of light brown sugar
- 1, 14 ounce can of pureed pumpkin
- 3 eggs

Ingredients for the glaze:

- 5 cups of powdered sugar
- 6 Tbsp. of whole milk

Directions:

1. Preheat the oven to 350 degrees. Grease a bundt cake pan and dust lightly with flour.
2. Prepare the cake. In a bowl, add in the cake flour, pumpkin pie spice, powdered espresso, dash of salt and baking powder. Stir well to mix.
3. In a separate bowl, add in the white sugar, light brown sugar and butter. Beat with an electric mixer until smooth in consistency. Add in the pureed pumpkin and eggs. Continue to beat until mixed. Add in the flour mix. Beat well until incorporated.
4. Pour into the cake pan.
5. Place into the oven to bake for 45 minutes or until baked through. Remove and set aside to cool completely.
6. Prepare the glaze. In a bowl, add in the whole milk and powdered sugar. Whisk until smooth in consistency. Drizzle over the top of the cake.
7. Slice and serve.

Toasted Pecan Bundt Cake

If you want to spoil yourself with something incredibly delicious, then this is the perfect bundt cake for you to prepare.

Makes: 12 to 16 servings

Total Prep Time: 1 hour and 30 minutes

Ingredients for the cake:

- 2 cups of pecans, chopped
- 3 cups of cake flour
- 1 tsp. of baking powder
- Dash of salt
- 1 cup of butter, soft
- 1 ¼ cups of light brown sugar
- ¾ cup of white sugar
- 4 eggs
- 2 Tbsp. of bourbon
- 1 tsp. of pure vanilla
- 1 cup of whole milk

Ingredients for the glaze:

- 4 ounces of cream cheese
- 3 Tbsp. of caramel sauce
- 1 cup of powdered sugar
- 2 to 3 Tbsp. of whole milk

Directions:

1. Preheat the oven to 350 degrees. Grease a bundt cake pan and dust lightly flour.
2. On a baking sheet, add a sheet of parchment paper. Add the pecans onto a baking sheet. Place into the oven to bake for 10 to 12 minutes or until toasted. Remove and set aside.
3. Prepare the cake. In a bowl, add in the cake flour, dash of salt and baking powder. Stir well to mix.
4. In a bowl of a stand mixer, add in the butter, light brown sugar and white sugar. Beat on the highest setting until fluffy in consistency. Add in the eggs, bourbon and eggs. Beat well to mix. Add in the flour mix. Continue to beat until just mixed. Add in ¾ of the toasted pecans. Fold well to incorporate.
5. Pour into the bundt cake pan.
6. Place into the oven to bake for 1 hour or until baked through. Remove and set aside to cool completely.

7. Prepare the glaze. In a bowl, add in the cream cheese and caramel. Beat with an electric mixer until smooth in consistency. Add in the powdered sugar and whole milk. Continue to beat until fluffy in consistency.
8. Pour the glaze over the top of the cake.
9. Sprinkle the remaining toasted pecans over the top.
10. Slice and serve.

Cinnamon Roll Bundt Cake

This is a bundt cake that tastes identical to homemade cinnamon rolls. It is the perfect bundt cake that you can serve in the morning during the weekend.

Makes: 10 to 12 servings

Total Prep Time: 1 hour and 20 minutes

Ingredients for the cake:

- ½ cup of butter, soft
- 1 ¼ cup of white sugar
- 3 eggs
- 2 ¼ cup of cake flour
- 2 tsp. of baking soda
- Dash of salt
- 1, .5 ounce pack of vanilla pudding mix
- ½ cup of sour cream
- 1 cup of whole milk
- 1 tsp. of pure vanilla
- 1/3 cup of pecans, chopped

Ingredients for the swirl:

- 2/3 cup of pecans, chopped
- 1 Tbsp. of powdered cinnamon
- ½ cup of butter, soft

Ingredients for the glaze:

- 4 ounces of cream cheese
- 2 cups of powdered sugar
- 2 to 3 Tbsp. of whole milk
- 1 tsp. of pure vanilla

Directions:

1. Preheat the oven to 350 degrees. Grease a bundt cake pan and dust lightly with flour.
2. In the bottom of the bundt pan, add in 1/3 cup of the chopped pecans. Set aside.
3. Prepare the cake. In a bowl, add in the cake flour, dash of salt, vanilla pudding mix and baking soda. Stir well to mix. Add in the sour cream, pure vanilla and whole milk. Stir well until mixed.

4. Prepare the swirl. In a bowl, add in the chopped pecans, powdered cinnamon and soft butter. Stir well to mix. Pour half of the swirl into the bottom of the cake pan. Pour the batter over the top. Pour the remaining swirl mix over the top. Swirl around with a knife.
5. Place into the oven to bake for 1 hour or until baked through. Remove and set aside to cool completely.
6. Prepare the glaze. In a bowl, add in the cream cheese, powdered sugar, whole milk and pure vanilla. Whisk until smooth in consistency. Drizzle over the top of the cake.
7. Serve immediately.

Banana and Peanut Butter Glaze Bundt Cake

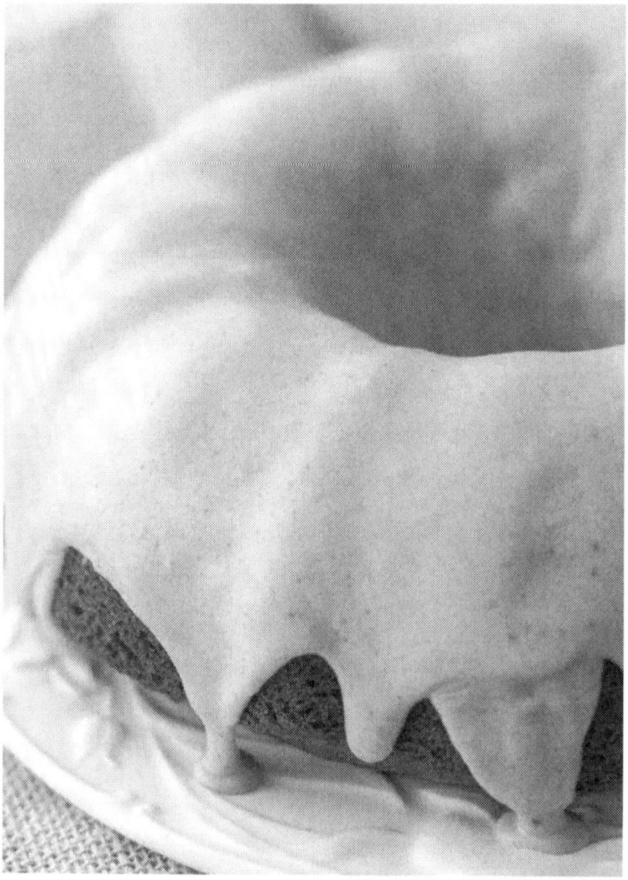

This is the perfect combination of two flavors that I know you won't be able to resist. It is sure to be a hit in your household.

Makes: 14 to 16 servings

Total Prep Time: 1 hour and 10 minutes

Ingredients for the cake:

- ½ cup of butter, soft
- 1/3 cup of white sugar
- 1 cup of light brown sugar
- 3 eggs
- 2 ¼ cups of cake flour
- 2 tsp. of powdered cinnamon
- 2 tsp. of baking soda
- Dash of salt
- ½ cup of sour cream
- ½ cup of bananas, mashed
- 2 tsp. of pure vanilla

Ingredients for the glaze:

- 2 to 3 Tbsp. of whole milk
- ¼ cup of smooth peanut butter
- ½ tsp. of pure vanilla
- 1 ½ cups of powdered sugar

Directions:

1. Preheat the oven to 350 degrees. Grease a bundt cake and dust lightly with flour.
2. Prepare the cake. In a bowl, add in the butter. Beat with an electric mixer for 1 minute or until fluffy in consistency. Add in the white sugar, light brown sugar and eggs. Beat again until mixed.
3. In a separate bowl, add in the cake flour, powdered cinnamon, dash of salt and baking soda. Stir well to mix. Add into the butter mix along with the mashed bananas, sour cream and pure vanilla. Beat well until just mixed.

4. Pour into the bundt pan.
5. Place into the oven to bake for 50 minutes or until baked through. Remove and set aside to cool completely.
6. Prepare the glaze. In a bowl, add in the whole milk, peanut butter, pure vanilla and powdered sugar. Whisk until smooth in consistency. Drizzle the glaze over the cake.
7. Allow to rest for 5 to 10 minutes or until the glaze is set.
8. Slice and serve.

Breakfast Bundt Cake

Just as the name implies, this is the perfect bundt cake to make for breakfast. It is so delicious, I know you will want to make it every morning.

Makes: 10 servings

Total Prep Time: 50 minutes

Ingredients:

- 2 cans of Pillsbury biscuits
- 5 eggs
- 1 cup of bacon bits
- 2 cups of cheddar cheese, shredded
- Dash of salt and black pepper
- ½ of an onion, chopped

Directions:

1. Preheat the oven to 350 degrees.
2. Slice the biscuits into 6 pieces. Transfer into a bowl.
3. In a separate bowl, add in the eggs and chopped onion. Season with a dash of salt and black pepper. Whisk until beaten. Pour over the biscuits.
4. Add in the bacon bits and shredded cheddar cheese. Stir well to mix.
5. Pour into a greased bundt cake pan.
6. Place into the oven to bake for 40 minutes or until golden.
7. Remove and serve.

S'mores Bundt Cake

With the help of this delicious bundt cake recipe, you will never have to go camping in order to enjoy the flavor of s'mores again.

Makes: 8 servings

Total Prep Time: 55 minutes

Ingredients for the cake:

- 1 box of chocolate cake mix
- 1 box of chocolate pudding
- 4 eggs
- ½ cup of vegetable oil
- ¼ cup of whole milk
- 1 cup of chocolate chips
- 8 to 10 marshmallows

Ingredients for the frosting:

- 4 cups of powdered sugar
- 1 stick of butter, soft
- 1/3 cup of whole milk
- 1 tsp. of pure vanilla
- Graham crackers, crushed
- 1 Hershey chocolate bar, broken into pieces

Directions:

1. Preheat the oven to 350 degrees. Grease a bundt cake pan and dust lightly with flour.

2. In a bowl, add in the chocolate cake mix, chocolate pudding, eggs, vegetable oil, whole milk and chocolate chips. Stir well until just mixed.

3. Add the marshmallows into the bottom of the bundt cake pan.

4. Pour the batter over the marshmallows.

5. Place into the oven to bake for 45 minutes or until baked through. Remove and set aside to cool completely.

6. Prepare the frosting. In a bowl, add in the powdered sugar, bust, whole milk and pure vanilla. Beat with an electric mixer until smooth in consistency. Pipe the frosting over the top of the cake.

7. Garnish the cake with the crushed graham crackers and pieces of the chocolate bar.

8. Slice and serve.

Pumpkin and Maple Bundt Cake

This bundt cake is incredibly moist and topped off with a glaze that everybody will fall in love with. It is the perfect dessert dish to serve during the holiday season.

Makes: 14 servings

Total Prep Time: 1 hour and 30 minutes

Ingredients for the cake:

- 1 cup of white sugar
- ¾ cup of light brown sugar
- 1 cup of vegetable oil
- 3 eggs
- 3 cups of cake flour
- 2 tsp. of baking soda
- 2 ½ tsp. of pumpkin pie spice
- Dash of salt
- 1, 14 ounce can of pureed pumpkin

Ingredients for glaze:

- 2 cups of powdered sugar
- 3 Tbsp. of whole milk
- 2 Tbsp. of maple syrup
- ½ cup of pecans, toasted and chopped

Directions:

1. Preheat the oven to 350 degrees. Grease a bundt cake pan and dust lightly with flour.

2. Prepare the cake. In the bowl of a stand mixer, add in the light brown sugar, vegetable oil and white sugar. Beat for 2 minutes or until creamy in consistency. Add in the eggs and pureed pumpkin. Continue to beat until mixed.
3. In a bowl, add in the cake flour, pumpkin pie spice, dash of salt and baking soda. Stir well to mix. Add into the sugar mix and continue to beat until just mixed.
4. Pour into the bundt cake pan.
5. Place into the oven to bake for 1 hour or until baked through. Remove and set aside to cool completely.
6. Prepare the glaze. In a bowl, add in the powdered sugar, whole milk and maple syrup. Whisk until smooth in consistency. Drizzle over the top of the cake.
7. Sprinkle the toasted pecans over the top.
8. Slice and serve.

White Russian Bundt Cake

This is a delicious bundt cake recipe that every adult in your household will fall in love with. Make this with freshly brewed coffee for the tastiest results.

Makes: 8 servings

Total Prep Time: 1 hour

Ingredients:

- 2 ¾ cups of cake flour
- 1 ½ tsp. of baking powder
- 1 tsp. of salt
- 1 cup of butter, soft
- 1 ½ cup of white sugar
- 4 eggs
- 2 tsp. of pure vanilla
- ¾ cup of whole milk
- ¼ cup of heavy whipping cream
- 1 cup of Kahlua liqueur

Ingredients for the glaze:

- 1 cup of powdered sugar
- 2 Tbsp. of Kahlua liqueur
- 3 Tbsp. of heavy whipping cream

Directions:

1. Preheat the oven to 325 degrees. Grease a bundt cake pan and dust lightly with flour.
2. Prepare the cake. In a bowl, add in the cake flour, dash of salt and baking powder. Stir well to mix.
3. In a separate bowl, add in the butter and white sugar. Beat with an electric mixer until fluffy in consistency. Add in the pure vanilla, eggs, whole milk, heavy whipping cream and Kahlua liqueur. Continue to beat until mixed. Add in the flour mix. Beat until just mixed.
4. Pour into the bundt cake pan.
5. Place into the oven to bake for 45 to 50 minutes or until baked through. Remove and set aside to cool completely.
6. Prepare the glaze. In a bowl, add in the powdered sugar, heavy whipping cream and Kahlua. Whisk until smooth in consistency. Drizzle over the top of the cake.
7. Slice and serve.

Coffee Bundt Cake

This bundt cake is incredibly moist and fluffy. It is infused with freshly brewed coffee and drizzle in a coffee glaze that you will want to make again and again.

Makes: 12 to 14 servings

Total Prep Time: 1 hour and 5 minutes

Ingredients for the cake:

- 3 cups of cake flour
- ½ tsp. of baking powder
- ½ tsp. of baking soda
- Dash of salt
- 4 eggs
- 1 ½ cups of light brown sugar
- 1 cup of butter, melted
- 1 cup of Greek yogurt
- 4 tsp. of instant coffee granules

Ingredients for the glaze:

- 1 cup of powdered sugar
- 1 tsp. of instant coffee granules
- 2 Tbsp. of boiling water

Directions:

10. Preheat the oven to 350 degrees. Grease a bundt cake and dust lightly with flour.
11. Prepare the cake. In a bowl, add in the cake flour, dash of salt, baking powder and soda. Stir well to mix.
12. In a separate bowl, add in the eggs and white sugar. Whisk until mixed. Add in the melted butter, Greek yogurt and instant coffee granules. Whisk well to mix. Add in the flour mix and fold gently to incorporate.
13. Pour into the bundt cake pan.
14. Place into the oven to bake for 50 minutes or until baked through. Remove and set aside to cool completely.
15. Prepare the glaze. In a bowl, add in the powdered sugar, instant coffee granules and boiling water. Whisk until smooth in consistency. Drizzle over the top of the cake.
16. Slice and serve.

Conclusion

Well, there you have it! Hopefully by the end of this cookbook, you have found plenty of bundt cake recipes that you can make with ease from the comfort of your own home. By the end of this bundt cake cookbook, not only do I hope you have found the confidence to make these moist cakes from scratch, but have over 25 bundt cake recipes that will help you do just that. So, what is next for you? The next step for you to take is to begin making all of these delicious bundt cake recipes for yourself. Once you have done that, don't hesitate to try preparing other bundt cake recipes you discover online. Good luck!

About the Author

Martha Stone is a chef and also cookbook writer. She was born and raised in Idaho where she spent most of her life growing up. Growing up in the country taught her how to appreciate and also use fresh ingredients in her cooking. This love for using the freshest ingredients turned into a passion for cooking. Martha loves to teach others how to cook and she loves every aspect of cooking from preparing the dish to smelling it cooking and sharing it with friends.

Martha eventually moved to California and met the love of her life. She settled down and has two children. She is a stay at home mom and involves her children in her cooking as much as possible. Martha decided to start writing cookbooks so that she could share her love for food and cooking with everyone else.

Author's Afterthoughts

Thank you for reading my book. Your feedback is important to us. It would be greatly appreciated if you could please take a moment to ***REVIEW*** this book on Amazon so that we could make our next version better

To receive an Email when there are "New Book Releases" by Martha Stone... Click on the "FOLLOW" box on the left hand side of Author Page. Register to be notified of new book releases. Be sure and scroll down to see any new books published or if another book could help you or someone you love.

Thanks!

Martha Stone

Printed by Amazon Italia Logistica S.r.l.
Torrazza Piemonte (TO), Italy

10521840R00059